2009

Down the Road the Children Go

Down the Road the Children Go

Dan Peters

For Carlos—
My student &
my teacher
Dan Pet
6/14

Blue Begonia Press   Yakima, Washington

Blue Begonia Press
225 So 15th Ave Yakima, WA 98902
bluebegoniapress.com

Library of Congress
Cataloging-in-Publication Data

Peters, Dan, 1968-
Down the road the children go / Dan Peters.
    p. cm.
ISBN-13: 978-0-911287-63-9 (alk. paper)
ISBN-10: 0-911287-63-9 (alk. paper)
I. Title.
PS3616.E839D69 2009
811'.6--dc22

2009038454

for Amy, Ella and Whit

&

for Doug and Marj Peters

Contents

PART FOUR: GENERAL AWARENESS

Down the road the children go,
a sister and a brother,
and they cannot help but wonder
at the beauty of the world.

—Maria Konopnicka

You Who Have Already Read These Poems,

A visiting, one of a kind (and I don't mean "unique"), poet-teacher at Iowa always said, "Always," and always smugly. "Always," said she who routinely missed class and office hours because of confabs and junkets, "always skip the first poem in a poet's book."

I bet you didn't, here. Four first poems, here. In four separate parts, here. Dan Peters doesn't repeat himself, here. Here, here, here, or here.

The first poem and last poem of each part of *Down the Road the Children Go* bookend experience which is connected and vital to the other parts of the book yet, importantly, remains separate.

To name names:
Part One: On the Other Side of This Door/Honey Dipper
Part Two: The Boatman's Dump/What Happened
Later That Day
Part Three: There's a Boy on the Bridge/The Florian Gate
Part Four: General Awareness/Blueberries and Ribs
I leave it to you and the poems of each part to give their experience a name.

Here, back to front, like an afterword in place of a foreword, like the epiphany of daily life, the world at large telescoping down to the moment at hand. Parts four, three, two, one.

Part four's "Blueberries and Ribs" plays off "General Awareness." It is good to know where we are and what's about us, in general. Peters is as deft with general awareness as John Prine is in "Lake Marie." Five or six storylines at once in the teller's tale, winding around each other for some reason we're waiting for. I can hear Prine asking, "You know what general awareness looks like on a road sign?! Caution! Gravel!" Gravel out where the asphalt ends, right down the middle of "the beauty of the world," as the epigraph goes. And Peters goes and, like Prine "out on the banks of old Lake Marie," he keeps his mouth shut, letting the details do the talking about general awareness. It's the dad, not Peters, in "General Awareness," who warns, "Look out there./... General awareness, guys./This is exactly what I've been talking about./You need to practice." The family in "Blueberries and Ribs" does. The family knows its home and neighbors and "the beauty of the world". The family's in the middle of it all. There is Iraq and one who has seen war who still comes home and feeds the people. Amazing. And there's the family that's been to the berry patch, enjoyed their buckets and gallons of berries for months, that now wants to share this patch with the one who's served while the family has feasted. General awareness, bringing the world home. This is everywhere in the closing part of this book.

Peters, also, knows the boy on the bridge leading into part three. That's not easy. It's not always a pretty sight. And, it's a long way to beauty and light and abundance at the Florian Gate in Krakow at the end of travel in part three. There are bumpy roads, here. Loose ends. Trouble. Failure. Things that don't get spread around, talked out, processed. Gravel. Blood. Broken glass. Accidents. Mystery. Voices. Romans. Christians. Nazis. Demolition. Agitation. Decay. Pain. Anger. Distances and gaps. And family, always family. And, finally, love and beauty and truth and empire at the Florian Gate. That's a roadmap that somehow leads to and passes through the historical site of a concentration camp, its gift shop, processing center/cafeteria, wall of death, and crematorium, to end, for now at least, at the Royal Way and a Christmas feast that a shirtless boy on a bridge would be hard-pressed to believe exists for him.

Truth and beauty, etc., we live with.

The chatty modern novelist laments the apple falling close to the tree. I'm tired of that. The apple falls.

I used to tell students that the times that pre-dated their births happened when they, the students, were out in the universe somewhere. Their faces would get all twisted-up. When Peters was out in the universe somewhere, he was headed in a pretty good direction. The apple falls.

Part two of *Down the Road the Children Go* may be the heart of the book. It certainly features the somewhere and family that Peters comes from. Old country carters, crofters. Innkeeepers. Sellers of coffee and spirits. Nightwatchmen. Gameskeepers. Servants. Then, Peters says, "They sailed away." They sure did. But, like their ancestors, they paid attention in order to get things carried, caught, grown, kept, sold, safe, and passed on, etc. They paid attention. This trait in the family tree, in *Down the Road the Children Go*, passes right on down to the poet's daughter and son, Ella and Whit.

In part two, we see it working in their parents and paternal grandparents, Papa and Grammy Peters. When Peters is six years old, his dad has the genius to show him, and take him through the heyday and demise of the old, local, and now defunct, calliope (read: Muse). Dan walks away from the experience listening to his dad whistling the old calliope's tunes under his breath. This is the dad who later tells his son, "We are journalists on the way to a party./Our assignment is to take notes,/report back." The dad who accompanies his son to the dump with coffees, to the art gallery, lecture hall, and night club. This is the son who accompanies his dad to the lake to bring the sailboat home. The son who is with him at the doctors' offices and hospitals. This is the son who will, in another context, quote his mom in order to describe his dad, "...your father is a big man./...your father was built to carry more." That's the way he reads, here.

And Grammy Peters. As individual as her husband, she shines throughout. She's the calm center. At the hospital. The smiling bride behind the veil in the car's rear window. The girl in Cathlamet on the basement stairs watching her father at his workbench standing over a swan he has killed. The four year old Peters tells his daughter about in 'Photograph of Your Grandmother in Bend," in the dead of winter, in the wagon, with the neighbor boys, "...lost in play. Making believe/in the cold air. Warm in the trust of these friends./Sure of the man who takes her picture." Grammy's, certainly, the ten year old in part two's first poem, "The Boatman's Dump," who is adrift with her brother in a rented boat at the center of Spirit Lake, looking overboard and through the clear, deep water, seeing the discarded outboard motors on the bottom, wondering, in what her son describes as a gift, a "dream," for the family: how to "float the treasure to the surface." Always at the center, attuned to the possiblities. Trusting, trustful.

How to get through? How to draw the best to us and with us?

Decades later, in "Above Quepos," Peters, remembering distant, unattainable lights and music during a night in a Costa Rican jungle, now, at home, faces the meaning of a grandmother's aging and a domestic night of lights and music floating up into a sky that is just as unreachable.

Closing part two, in "What Happened Later That Day," with the same desire to ascend, to "float the treasure to the surface," Peters, again the poet paying attention to what's at hand (in this case, himself and the landscape near his home), celebrates the memory of his grandmother in the rising mist, blue sky, clouds, hills, and, speaking for the family, in "our slow breath."

The moment at hand. The family we make from who we are and, as Lovins would say, what we have to work with. The family that experiences, as Gary Snyder says, what we pass on. Part one of *Down the Road the Children Go*. The moment at hand.

Amy and Dan Peters both married well. What we see here of the married life, before babies, shows us that. Pre-baby, after the first ultrasound, Dad's asking all the crazy questions (read: questions parents ask, pre-baby and forever). Mom's there with Dad. In the rain in Fremont. With Gran at Highgate. Making the big plans with him "on that long drive,/at the end of the day somewhere in the North Cascades." Mom and Dad are a couple.

The moment at hand. Not so easy to talk about, so likely to write well about, as Peters does, here. Everyone's take and detail on the moment at hand are different, difficult, and freshly conceived. Things haven't fully sifted through, yet. There is "this," and there is "that." This and that's *Down the Road the Children Go*, part one.

Parents and children (child, ME/OE, cild, akin to Goth, kilthei: womb/read: source of it all!) are, he said, Multitudinous! Vulnerable. Repentant. Innocent. Responsible (to and for). Somehow larger than life. Afraid. Curious. Forgiving. At their stations, Bodeen would remind us. Individual and Family. When parents are honest, they're as full of wonder as the children they're raising. The car backs into the garage door. There is a skunk, maybe two, in the window well. A story, maybe two, in the past. Kisses and hugs. Empty beds, crowded beds. Tap Water. Acrimony and cheese. No lie. No blinking red Story Time. No tuna fish sandwiches. Instead, "Golden Slumbers" at bedtime and telling stories and homemade popsicles tomorrow.

Moment (L., momentum, movement, to move) to moment to moment at hand. Now, while it's happening. Parent and child. Getting that down. Part one. Hang on, boy, Mom whispers. I'm right here. Dad puts the crow's beak in his mouth, squeezes down, and smiles when you caw back. Dad wondering when he gets home, wondering where you'll be this time on the other side of this door. Moment to moment to moment. Together and apart. Bullfrog and bumblebee, horse and rider, and Mom.

And that magic, better than a falling down barn ten feet off the ground somewhere, is the family, the home.

Amy, wife, mother, magician on this particular morning, pancake-maker, woman with spoon and bowl writing "in the slow language of honey" dripping across the surface of the batter, contemplates, articulates, the possibility of finding "their whole story," the family's story.

The magic's in the domestic.

Four, three, two, one.

Down the road the children go.

Barry Grimes
The Riverhouse
August 2009

Part One

ON THE OTHER SIDE OF THIS DOOR

You haven't always run to greet me. At first,
you were unable to walk, indifferent
to the sound of the garage door, intent on food, sleep.

Then, I could hear feet pound
through the kitchen as I approached.
I'd open the door, you'd run into my arms.

Now, you hide. You want to surprise me.
Nobody's there. Hello? I say,
and you pop out of the bathroom, from behind a wall.

We tricked you! you say, eyes shining.
Someday—merciful god, make today last—
you'll hear me coming and we'll go back to the start.

Ultrasound, Number 1

What if I have nothing to say about you?
What if I can't tell you what I know?
What if you make me get religion,
 turn on my friends and stop being funny?
What if you never change anything?
What if I get greedy, long for safety, join a service club?
What if you hate baseball?
What if I slam a door? Shout shit?
What if I have to love musicals, or swim meets, or tattoos?
What if you get me back?
What if you see through me before I see through you?
What if I get tired, later?
What if we want the same thing?

Everything I Touch I Explain
in My Head to My Child

Gran doesn't know where she is.
Over the phone she says, *I'm down the street*
from where I used to live.

She thinks she's been moved.
I get in the car and back out of the garage.
This is how long it takes me.

She's in her room. The caller ID: M Johnson.
I call the home and they tell me,
We'll send someone to check on her.

Whatever way it works out, this is hard.

When I get there, I go straight up.
I say, You are safe. This is your room.
Everything is ok. You did the right thing

by calling. You were confused.
But that's impossible, she says.
It must have been an hallucination.

But why? Maybe the medicine.
It might be getting older. She nods.
That might be it. We talk about grandchildren,

great-grandchildren and our pregnancy.
She remembers childhood.
Gran looks at me and says,

I've tried to stay ready. I am ready.

And Yesterday

last day of summer

Amy and I visit Gran.
She's in her new room.
Same facility, different care.
She eats with her regular table.
She received two bird feeders
for a house warming.
I'll have them in stereo, she says.
She talks to us as always.
Amy shows her profile,
Gran tells us about Hal and Mom.
When we leave, Amy says,
*I come here expecting one thing
and it's always different.*

In the Roundabout

Rain taps on the car roof while I wait.
Miles going with a mute and the tack of castanets.
Sketches of Spain. Hazards on. Any minute,

Amy will reach for the door and startle me.
When I close my eyes, thinning tree limbs
gesture in front of streetlights. It's the wind,

but it looks like people are running by me in the dark.
When I open my eyes, the windshield's covered in rain
and there is a big yellow leaf from under the Fremont Bridge

plastered on the blue hood of the car.
Miles winding down and up.
I parked near the bridge. Coffee and essays

at the Still Life Café. Rain pounded the skylights.
Lightning and thunder on my way out.
I don't want any of this to end.

Now I'm waiting. Many beats, then none.
Drops are blown from needles or finally catch enough
and land on the roof of the car at random.

As it turns out, I see Amy a long way off,
twist the ignition, release the brake
and click silent the blinkers.

Amy's here. Miles, gone.
And tonight's half moon
moves fully from the clouds.

Bird in My Hand

January 21ˢᵗ, 2004

I wake up at 6:30, an hour before sunrise.
I feel my chest tighten with a cold I can't shake.
When I cough, I see spots.
I drink two shots of expired Robitussin.

In ten minutes I feel different.
I walk to the bathroom,
kneel down and wait.
I let both cats out and fall on the couch.

An hour after dawn I walk into the kitchen.
Our cats are on the sill.
One of them has brought a bird.
She has never done this.

I grab a grocery bag. The body
rolls off the ledge. Its weight
barely pulls the plastic. I come inside
and see your mom, still carrying you.

I say nothing of the omens I've seen and felt.
On the way to the hospital
we talk about when payday is.
We decide to use the checkbook.

We promise to love you
as much as we love each other.
At 10 to 10 we pull into Memorial
and by 11:30, you are here.

That night, we read to you,
play Greg Brown for you.
The next morning, I drive home
and send pictures out into the world.

On my way back to the hospital
at the start of your second twenty-four hours,
I look to my left and see a boy in a little yellow bus
chewing on his coat collar and waving at me.

He picks me out for some reason
and twists around in his seat. He's staring.
For a moment I wonder, Why is he on this bus?
Is there something wrong with the boy?

Is there something special about this child?
Below his smiling face, the word EPIC.
I raise my arm and wave as he pulls away.
My hand, a wing above the wheel.

From the Basement, On the Road

Two years ago, on an afternoon like this one,
slow moving, early spring sunshine,
your mom and I sat down and decided we wouldn't
turn away from you anymore. It was time.

We were finally ready. But we weren't.
When the conversation ended,
I worked on school stuff by myself.
I heard your mom relearning "Clair De Lune"

on the piano in the basement.
The notes began—hesitant, distant.
The chords drifted in the vents. Each time,
the sound grew surer, came closer.

One year ago, on an evening like this one,
the days stretched slightly, a chance of snow,
we drove to Winthrop to stay with friends.
We talked the whole five hours.

As we drove along the Columbia and the Methow,
we approached the subject sensibly.
This caution may have been a fault but
we understood anything could happen.

No matter what comes, it's right, now.
That's what we were waiting for.
I wanted you to know this while you learn to smile.
While you are still more animal than girl.

I wanted to tell you, Ella, your mom and I are sure.
It's a sense that settled in on that long drive,
at the end of the day somewhere in the North Cascades.

One Month, One Day

You fell asleep in my arms last night.
I was playing Kennedy's inaugural.
It was exactly forty-three years before you were born.
You closed your eyes in the dark of the den.

Twice they opened, saw me, and closed again.
After Kennedy's speech,
I placed you at the foot of our bed.
You have dark blue eyes. Lots of reddish hair.

You have my chin, your mother's lips, the flat nose
of the breast-fed. This is nothing.
We don't know what to make of you yet.
And the obvious part is almost over.

Frost read at Kennedy's inaugural. He'd brought a poem
but the sun's glare made it impossible to read.
So he recited "The Gift Outright" from memory.
Yesterday, it rained here in Selah and in Yakima, where I teach.

At 11:32 I told my class you were one month old.
I told them how you backed into the world.
It won't be long, Ella. You respond to the light.
You hear the rain, same as me.

It's been one month, one day. This is what passes between us.
Your memory, my voice, flashes
of what's to come, what we withhold,
light sleep, what we do for each other,

what you see of me in the dark when your lids part,
what we ask of each other.
Let whatever is weak in me be surrendered.
Our work, like the sun, such as it is, will find us.

This Goddamn Eye Thing

I meet them getting off the 5:05. They've been up in the air
all day. Sylvia in front of Dick as they leave the gate.
When I wave, she waves back. I hold my hand out.

Welcome Grandma and Grandpa.
Did you have a nice trip down? Could you see Rainier?
Sylvia points out their bags and I grab them from the pile.

I put the bags in the back of the car and drive home
the scenic way. We park in the garage and Sylvia walks
through the narrow path flanked by the car, the mower

and the baby jogger. Dick, walking between us,
turns just before entering the house and says,
You'll have to forgive me, Dan.

I've got this goddamn eye thing. You may have heard about it.
I have to go slower. Inside, Amy holds Ella.
Sylvia touches her cheeks, looks into her eyes.

Dick rocks on his feet, smiles, and waits to see.

On the Morning of the Last Day of School

The man walked every street on his hill. It was half-light. Before the news hit the front steps, and so he walked slowly down the middle of fifth and all other roads. He took a cup of coffee. He had his camera in his pocket. Carrying something gave him a purpose, made him feel normal. One year ago today, also before dawn, he woke alone on a strange couch and drove home, his feet bare and covered in mud. As he climbed the long hill, the man felt an ache in the back of his legs that wasn't there when he pushed his daughter up the same rise. A week ago, his cat disappeared. Let out and never returned. Now, quail walked the yard on mornings like this. The man turned at the top of the hill and looked toward Selah Ridge. He caught his breath as he took a few sunrise shots. It was a year since his last drink. It was two months since he knew he'd never drink again. One since he'd said this out loud. It hadn't been hard. The man just stopped.

He could only remember a few times it had been dicey. New Year's Eve he drank seven diet cokes while his high school friends had Busch Lights. There had been a few dinners missing red wine. Camping, early on. A hot trip down the river. But he measured the time in months, not days. Two months ago, he'd seen his friend handcuffed on the bumper of a squad car. Seen his friend's face. The evidence bag in the morning: broken glasses, a game ticket, a birth announcement. This was it for him. A month later, he heard himself tell a student, I don't drink anymore.

The man went slowly down the hill. Pairs of garbage cans lined his route. He came to his house and kept walking. He crossed Crusher Canyon, stepped over an irrigation ditch and on to a large vacant tract. The side of a hill was cut away at one edge, leaving a wall of rock and dirt. Some time soon there would be houses, the man thought. This might be someone's backyard, or living room. The sun was just up. He sat on a rock and stared. He was sure no one could see him from the road. The face of the cliff was unsettled and exposed. From time to time, small slides trickled down the wall. Half way up, sparrows had built homes in the cliff. Holes they'd dug and lived in. They'd been there as long as the man could remember. This morning, the birds were in constant motion above his head. There were too many to count. He watched a long while. They came and went, fed on something too small to see.

The man closed his eyes. He knew the birds were still there and he knew he was alone. School kids would cross this lot some time later, after he was gone. He'd be warm in the shower by then, or he'd be watching his daughter stir in her crib. She would never know that other person, he thought. He opened his eyes and tried to picture those children as they passed beneath the layers of mudflow, reworked ash, and streambeds. He imagined them as they walked by all that stone eroded and dealt out again by rivers. But for now, it was just the man, those bands of earth and a thousand swallows.

10th Anniversary Letter to Amy

Let's make this our 10th Anniversary *Year*. Like it's a hundred.
Why not? Let's spend the year getting shined up. Like the
Olympics or the elections are coming. Build new stadia. World
class accommodations for even the esoteric events. Synchro-
feeding, maybe. We'll tax the shit out of ourselves. This is our
chance to remake the city. Not that our bonds need it, but we
will aim to restore their glory and update communication. Add
mass transit for this love. We'll make it all back on good will.
Feather the nest, not line the pockets. Classy, with a loveable
mascot. We will change the way we are seen. We'll invite the
world. Ramp up. Light that fucking flame and start running.

Here's what I mean: The Summer of the Bug (this very
summer) has been a prelude to the prelude. The Year of the
Peters doesn't sound right. In any case, we are at the beginning
of three hundred and sixty-five days of connubial pride.
We want to do it right.

Imagine a reality show is following us for the year, tracking
our progress. Cameras everywhere. But we won't ignore them.
This year, we'll learn to keep the camera in mind. We'll act like
the whole world is watching this house. Live like Ella is taking
notes. We will be proud of our actions in this tenth year. Feel
good about the way we sleep. We are playing for the Pontiac
Aztec. Immunity is riding on it. We are the stars and we have
not forgotten it. The reunion show—no matter how they edit
the footage— will be clips of you bumping into things and me
dancing for Ella and Ella chasing the cat, screaming.

Just so you know—and to get us started—after you left, Ella
and I played on the kick-n-kick, read *Look and Listen, Hop on
Pop*. She was in a great mood—tired, but not upset. The tired
where she lays on her back and listens to you read and looks at
the pages carefully. And sometimes at you. The tired where she
rests her hand on my forearm as I read. Now she's asleep in her

swing. The room is dark and she is holding her blanket up to her nose, playing with the tags.

Just when life can't get any better.

We'll call it The Year of Delight.

My Daughter's First Baby Doll

never sleeps.
She is always happy,
tan, pink, molded, sewn,
blue-eyed and full of sand.

Skunk in the Well

I'd come to believe that this child made me even.
I saw her whiteness as my own. Then one morning,
at the end of our first summer—long walks
through the neighborhood, neighbors smiling,
me smiling back—a father and his son arrive at my door
and place a trap in my window well.

The skunk dropped in over night.
I watched its muddied tail
sweep across the small basement window
while my child slept upstairs.
I went to the book and I called the man.
He said, *Sit tight.* I did just that.
Through the monitor, I heard Ella stir in her crib.
The animal paced around, sniffed the air,
searched my bright basement with its black eyes.

That morning as Ella and I played on the floor
I listened to the animal grow desperate.
I could hear it claw the glass over and over.
It tried to tunnel out.
A hole formed at the base of the concrete half circle.
When I went outside and looked down the well, it was gone.
Curled up asleep or burrowing deeper into the soft ground.

Within minutes, a truck backed into our driveway.
The man was fit, clean, compact and handsome.
Blond, close cut hair and mustache.
He smiled and shook my hand.
His teenage son rolled out wearing a black concert shirt.
The father took a long knife from his truck
and asked where it was.
The three of us walked around back, Ella in my arms.
He stood over the well, then knelt beside it.
He set the knife on the ground and braced himself

before bending half his body into the hole.
I can't see him, he said when he emerged.
He went back to the truck for a cage and a tin of cat food.
He leaned in again and set the trap.
It'll get hungry, he said when he resurfaced.
Call me when it hits.

The cage lay empty all day and night.
No movement. No sign.
In the morning, the skunk was in the trap.
Ella was not yet up. I made the call.

The father and son returned.
We cleared a path from the backyard to his truck.
The father said, *Why don't we settle up*
before I get him outta there?
Whatever he said, I paid.
He took a small blue tarp from his cab
and cut a slit in the center.
The father put on rubber gloves,
reached the tarp into the well.
We were still and silent.
He drew his arm out, the handle of the cage
held through the slit in the tarp.
Not yet knowing what was next, not having asked,
I looked at them out of the side of my eye.
The scene was tender.
He tucked the blue plastic around the cage with care.
He was gentle because he had to be.
We looked at the cage and at each other.

He closed the tarp with thin white masking tape. A gift.
The son waved and climbed back into the cab.
Without prompting, the father took off his gloves,
walked over to me and shook my hand.
We whispered a few words back and forth—thanks, mainly—
and the three of them drove away.

Inside, the house vibrated. Differently.
I should feel absolved. Should feel free.
But now, I feel the presence of the skunk.
I try to imagine how it fell in the first place.
I wonder what it did all day,
dug deep in the cool earth beneath my house.
Alone again with my daughter, I question its fate.

A week later, another skunk, a child,
falls in the same place at the same time.
It leaps out and disappears.
I question if it was ever there.
And I am left to wait for the next thing to drop in the well.
It may be that I am meant to attract
snakes and mice and young skunks to our door,
that what came before is not forgiven
but returns, juvenile, potent.

Umptanum Creek Settlement

Up the canyon to Umptanum Creek.
Yellow snuggly, purple backpack.
We cross the river on a swaying bridge.
The canyon is narrow. We have it to ourselves.
Some trails go to the ridge.
We hike the slope of the creek.
Here and there, beaver dams.
You play with my hair.

Burnt posts loosely wrapped in barbed wire.
Nothing much. A wide flat spot. Green.
Old pear and apple trees. Faint rows.
I don't know who lived here. Today,
it's just the three of us—a new family.
This is where we turn around.

Close to the bridge, we're stopped by a train.
Your mouth open, face flush with cold.
Calm to the last car.
We move up the tracks.
Hear the engine going up the Yakima.
I touch the rail. Nothing.
We look down the line, eyes level.
We bounce over the river, home.

Her First Ten Months, Her First Three Words

Ella says *mama* and *da*.
Says her first name, *ay-ya*. Spanish
feminine pronoun, third person.
We have so many pictures of Ella
things have begun to blur together.

Ella is Amy's daughter.
Amy is Sylvia's daughter.
Sylvia is Ruth's daughter.
Ruth is Eli's daughter.
Eli moved to Alaska from Norway.
She was the only mother
at the Deadwood Creek gold camp.
She lived a hard life.
We have one picture of Eli.
She delivered Ruth alone,
downstream in Dawson.

Ella is Dan's daughter.
Dan is Marj's son.
Marj is Mary's daughter.
Mary is Mary Ella's daughter.
Mary Ella married Daniel, a carpenter
with no head for business.
We have one picture of Mary Ella.
She's posing in a funny hat with a feather.
She could've run the family, Mary says,
if Daniel would've let her.

The Inside and Outside Lights

are on, two days before the sun turns around,
ten minutes to five. No one knows what we will eat tonight.
Amy has one more meeting. Ella's up from the crib.
I have spent the afternoon on the couch.
A Pendleton blanket shielding my eyes from the shining tree.

Goodbye Donkeys,

Ella says to the elk herd on New Year's Day.
There was a party at the coroner's office, New Year's Eve.
Lights on in the old Pizza Hut. Shades up in the front rooms.
A few people moving around.

Notice six things a day. If this seems sad, you might be sad.

At the restaurant, there's a man in a tan leather jacket.
Greased hair. On the scene. He leans against the door jam.
Behind him, on a bench near the exit, is a woman all in white.
White nylon coat trimmed in white fur. Legs crossed
and bouncing nervously. She looks into the distance.

Amy says, *There is nowhere to escape.*

Two doors up, New Year's Eve, huge, illegal fireworks,
shower people at the party in sparks.
Every few minutes, another two or three.
Like they weren't working right, or being lit by hand.
Deep thoops, followed by bangs and crackles.
Loud and full of light. Somebody says, *Maybe you should stop.*
And another guy shouts, *No. Do it Greg!* And thoop.
The guy who shouted laughs hysterically.
He gets people to chant, *Greg, Greg, Greg, Greg,*
until another one goes off. He laughs just as hard every time.
Someone lies and says the cops are coming.

When you begin to notice, there's more to notice.
Still, this seems like a dream.
So, goodbye donkeys.
The sun is shining just after a nap.

Tap Water

I broke the water pitcher. Bumped it off the counter.
Also, I snore. We are expecting a child in March.
I drink tap water and sleep on the couch
this third week of the new year.
I get into bed sometimes, early in the morning.
The water tastes the same. Good.
It isn't as cold but it isn't forever.

Two Red Peppers

Opened, the two peppers reveal
two more peppers, green and red pearls,
growing within.
The first, just months before Ella.
And now another. A pepper in a pepper.
Curved like a sleeping child.
Ella reaches in gently.
It is, we agree, a good sign.
She puts it up to her open lips.
Her teeth. And we say, softly, *no, no, no.*

Everyone Talks About the Wind

coming tonight. It's supposed to start soon and keep coming.
My first poem for you is my last poem for my students.
Tonight we'll walk away from the classroom together.
It will not be hard to see. We'll go past the softball fields
and through a neighborhood to a garden in the middle
of the city. You'll be fifteen blocks west, Whitman.

We'll stop and put our work where anyone can see it.

It's still winter, Whit. Two feet coming as late as you are early.
We'll notice more than six things. Church bells. Big waves
and small. A man's little corner of the world.
Keep telling me to slow down. Say, You'll never get it, Dad,
if you don't slow down. Tonight we will hear
the wind in the grass, the wind on the face of a cliff.

The Man Who Lived Twice

I'd weep too, Jesus, bringing a man
dead four days back to this world.

But at the first ballgame of the year,
Ella hugs Boomer, the mascot. Her cousins,
her grandma and grandpa. Her mom and dad.
Her new brother. All of them with her at the park.
She cries when she leaves the game early. She's two.

No one can say how much longer Lazarus lived.
He died twice, I guess, leaving his family a second time.

My son's swing tock, tock, ticks.
It's set to stop after a time.
Sometimes he stays asleep.
Sometimes the stopping wakes him.

Three Stories from My Son's First Year

1.

Last summer we threw a party for Barry's retirement. People came over to help set up. Lovins was there. He'd never been to our house. He looked south through the gap and said, *You got a great view of Rattlesnake Ridge.* No, I said, That's Ahtanum. As soon as I said it, I knew I was wrong. I was sure it was Ahtanum. I told lots of people, That's Ahtanum. No one ever said it wasn't. I looked it up on maps. But I was wrong. I called that distant ridge the wrong name for years.

2.

There's a mural in the basement of our house. A beach scene in the bedroom put up by the former owners. We moved our office into this room to make way for our son's crib upstairs. Bookshelves. A desk and computer. I worked there all spring and summer.

At the end of summer, and after we'd been living in the house for six years, Amy and I are in the basement during naptime. We talk about the mural. It's a white sand beach. Jungle up to the edge. Coconut trees over the shoreline. The water is blue and the break is small. I say, It's just perfect for this room. *I know,* Amy says. *Don't you just want to go live in that house?* What house? Amy closes the door. Behind it, there, back in the palms, clearly visible, a house I'd never seen.

3.

I wrote a poem for Amy that says: *There's a ridgeline that runs from pane/to pane/in front of our house./I love you like that.* Since writing those lines, a gravel mine has eaten into the hill below the ridge. For years, I have looked out our window and hated what I saw. At night, when I saw their lights. During the day, heavy digging equipment. I hated the whole operation. It took over my view.

Late last summer, pushing our children in a stroller along the top of our hill, I felt a huge boom and another part of the ridge became a cloud and a rock slide. It was being crushed. The pit was growing. I stopped to watch the dust rise and descend.

I looked around. It was an otherwise beautiful day.

A Long and a Short Walk on Your First Birthday

It was like most days. I got home from school and your mom left for work. We goofed around in the living room. You pulled yourself up on the ottoman over and over. Then you walked four feet away from it and fell. Your first steps.

I put you and Ella in the stroller. We crossed Crusher and walked the flat lot where the birds live in the cliff face. This is a new way, I said. *It's okay*, your sister said, *I'll be brave.* I knew where we were headed, but I didn't know if there was a way out. At the other end of the lot the dirt turned to road again. Here we go, I said. It was 8th. And before I knew it, we came out next to the first house I remember.

I lived a year on that dead end street when I was Ella's age. A rented house, one level, sliding glass door in the back. I slept in a crib in the same room as Rod, throwing beanbag frogs at each other at night. Also—a fork in an outlet, Uncle Hal giving me a sip from his beer can, his cigar in the same hand, the elastic net baseball return, "Jeremiah Was a Bullfrog", being dared to kiss the Madisen girl, hand painted ornaments, hide and seek until dark, the hydrant, home base.

We didn't stop, didn't slow down. Two girls played basketball in the driveway. A teenager got in a car and took off around us. I wasn't completely sure it was the right house until we'd gone a block. We went back to Crusher and up the steep hill to our house. It made the afternoon go right by. When we returned there were other things to do. There was a party. Dinner to make. I even forgot to tell your mom about your first steps until our friends were there. That's how things go, Whit. Fast. I wanted you to have this afternoon we had together.

Her Hands and Mine

My arms are almost too much to lift
mornings when I pull on an undershirt.
My knuckles give out when I carry my child
wrong on the way to the mailbox.

Each morning I count the pills.
When the bottle stops rattling
my fingers grow numb overnight.
At my daughter's open door

I see her sleeping in her new bed.
When I shift my sore feet,
her eyes flutter beneath their lids,
her fingers grab at something in her dream,

untouched by her father's weak grip.

Acrimony and Cheese

On my way home I pay $55.57 to fill up. My wife tells me she'll know by Friday if she still has a job. The three year old asks for acrimony and cheese for lunch then shits her pants and pees on the rug. My dad says, *Sometime, when you have a minute, I want to talk to you about your relationship with your brother.* The one year old hits himself with a broom, falls into a chair leg, gets to his feet and is pushed to the floor by his sister. By the time it's over, he has his first bloody nose to go with his first fever. My wife picks him up. *Naptime,* she says, dabbing his nose. Sometime he cries when I put him down, I tell her. She walks away without saying anything. He won't today, I add. He does. From the haze of my own sleep, I hear my wife open and close and open and close doors in various parts of the house. When I wake up, I look around. She's backed into the garage door again. It's three quarters closed, bumped from its track and going nowhere.

Storytime

Your mom points to the book and says,
That b-o-o-k is going in la baSUra.
I say something about it being a gift from a friend.
Yeah, thanks friend, she says.
Here's what she tells me:
It's predawn. You are nursing in the dark living room.
Your face is relaxed and your breathing deep.
You drift, hand tucked against your chest.
Nearly on the other shore.
Ten feet away, the book, a gift for your first birthday,
turns itself on.
Red lights blink and a female voice calls out, It's Storytime!
Your mom can't move with you on her lap.
She grits her teeth. The woman in the book
says it again and again.
Eighty times, your mom tells me.
The voice wakes you up.
Hang on, boy, your mother's voice whispers.
I'm right here. It'll be over soon. Soon enough.

After Your First Night in Bed

You won't always sleep so well.
You won't always lie on top of the blanket, sideways.
You'll miss the crib.
You'll outgrow this bed, too.
You can't jump from one end to the other.
You can't sleep with us.
You can open the door and walk down the hall.
You can fall out.
You won't always be alone.
You'll have different dreams.
You can't go back.
Starting this morning,
you rise as you wish.

Squeezing the Crow

I put the crow's beak in my mouth,
bite down on the soft stuffed vinyl.
I swing it slowly back and forth.
You love this trick, your dad's clowning.

We work on nose and mouth.
I point to mine. Here's my mouth.
Where's your mouth? You make a knuckle,
rub your nose, screw up your face and sigh.

You had your shots this morning.
Your mother asked the doctor, *What should he be saying?*
Three words, Whit. Three more than you know.
It's too soon to worry. There's time.

You put a finger in your mouth
take it out and stick it in mine.
You look away. Walk a few steps.
Crawl to the birds. Change the subject.

Before her nap, your sister says *Mouth, Whit. Boca.*
Once she's down, it's just the two of us.
You wave and clap. You know your name and *No.*
I don't know if you know *Dad.*

Mouth. Eye. Ear. Bird. Where's the bird, Whit?
I pick up the Audubon Western Meadowlark
a gift for your first Christmas
and press its middle until it sings.

You take up the Song Sparrow,
throw it over your head with a flick.
I stop the questions.
Put the House Wren and sparrow in one hand,

swallow in the other. I toss them in the air
like large tennis balls. As they come around,
I clutch them to activate their buried calls.
When I do it right, all three sing at once.

Your laugh makes me laugh.
I lose my concentration and they land on the carpet.
I reach for the crow put the beak in my mouth again.
I hold it out for you to bite. You lean in

and carefully kiss the black bird.
I give it a squeeze. It caws. You caw back.

Before Christmas

I'm driving. Ella and Whit are in back.
Ella, who's three, asks,
Do your wishes come true?
What do you mean, honey?
When you wish, does it come true?
Sometimes, I say. Why? *I don't know.*
I can see her in the mirror, thinking.
She looks out the window and says,
Maybe it's because summer comes and goes.

Summer Solstice

The boy in the mirror is you.
You're in my left arm.
We're in the bathroom off the kitchen.

Your left arm is extended.
You tilt forward, grab an edge
of the medicine cabinet and pull.

The mirror pops open.
Shaving cream, razor, a brush.
The door bounces back, returns to your hand.

You grip the frame,
swing it back and forth.
There and not there.

There's half of you. All of me.
The razor again. Ok, I say, ok.
I close the mirror. There we are, smiling.

This Is How It Starts

for Ella turning four

Last summer you learned the difference
between a bumble and a honey bee
between a wasp and a bald-faced hornet.
You said, *I smell rain.* Asked,
Is that how it starts, Mama?

You call your brother *Buddy,*
tell strangers, *He's a bit mischievous.*
You hold his hand, bring him
your least favorite toys.

This fall, we share afternoons
while Mom works and Whit naps.
Time is slow. I fight to stay with it.
We go downstairs or to your room.
We feed and bathe our babies.
Go on a whale hunt.

In the spring you changed beds.
It's hard. You don't have to say sorry.
It's each of us shaping all of us.
I tuck you in. Tell stories.
Sing "Golden Slumbers." The cat curls up.
Your mom and I sit on the couch.
She's with you in the mornings.
Waking, dressing, school, the library.
She's got the stories.
She recalls beautiful flashes.
It's something you've given her.
Your mom remembers exactly what she loves.
She tells me every day.

The First Campfire

Your father won't lie. These are stories.
The bible is a story. Unicorns are a story.

There was a flood.
People tell stories about it.

That doesn't mean
they're just stories.

The stars over your bed absorb light all day.
When we close your door at night, they glow.

We hung them there. You can count them.
They will always come out the same.

The stars in the sky are planets and suns.
Like our sun, only very far away.

You can count them.
They will never come out the same.

Shooting stars
are a different story.

I was younger than Whit
when men walked on the moon.

They drove around, like your book shows.
Planted a flag and parachuted home.

The flares over the firing center look like stars,
but they aren't. They parachute to earth, too.

They show where men hide.
Show others how to find them.

That doesn't mean
the night is any less a mystery.

One last story. The stars in the sky
are from the first campfire.

People rose out of the ground.
They were afraid of the dark.

So they made a big fire and the sparks
went up and stayed there.

Traces filled the sky like these stars fill your room.
And the people were less afraid.

Catch

I chase Whit to the basement at bedtime.
He's in the dark across the threshold,
at the edge of the light from the stairwell.
He turns around and I can just make out his smile.
We get our breath. He walks toward me,
his face growing brighter. He reaches out
and shuts the door. I listen for what happens next.

Close One Eye

After the blessing,
Ella extends her arm.
She holds her hand up,
palm out, directly
in front of her face.
She squints an eye,
keeps the other open
and blocks me from sight.
It's a trick we've all tried.
Now you're here.
Now you're not.
Amy says, *Ella,*
what are you doing?
Please stop that.
Ella is smiling.
She moves her hand
and one by one
aims to shut us out.

My Brother's Closet

We get the marbles down.
They were Dad's then Rod's then mine.
They've been up there thirty years.
Whit digs in the shoebox with both hands.
Cat's eyes and steelies clink.
I look on the highest shelf.
Plastic fraternity tumblers.
Homecoming pictures. Catcher's mask.
Cheryl Tiegs on *Sports Illustrated*.
A baseball team picture.
Pennants. Cub Scout badges.
A jackknife. Dice.
I dig for a small black frame
at the bottom of the pile.
It's a real monarch butterfly.
I take it down to show Ella.
You remember Uncle Rod?
This was Uncle Rod's.
Whit raises his hands to hold it,
his fingers filled with puries.

Leap Day

for Amy

When you are sorrowful, look again in your heart, and you shall see that in truth you are weeping for that which has been your delight.
Khalil Gibran

I've hated that gravel pit for years. Hated it as much as I love the ridge it's in. I've told you this. I love its changes. The snow covered smoothness, early spring Irishness, late spring redness. But mostly, I love its constancy. Then, six folds from the gap, they started digging. Fucking progress. Fuck. It was like they were doing something directly to me, to us, every time I heard a boom and saw dust rise. I let it get to me. And I look out at it every day. I've even hatched plans—sugar in the tanks, lawsuits, pulling up stakes—but there isn't anything I can do to defend the ridge against the people who own the rights.

The past few mornings I've been looking out the new doors. It's the last thing I do before I put on my coat and go. I'm trying to get a feel for the kitchen, for things working. It's strange isn't it? These nice things. I sit at the table, put in my contacts and look out the glass doors. A couple of days ago I was there when the sun broke over the horizon, surprising me. Yesterday, it was clouds across the valley. Low and opposite the house. Today, I sat thinking about the pit. I slipped and called it a gravel mine. Fucking gravel mine, I thought. That's it. It's not a pit, it's a mine. It's not destruction. The more they cut, the more we see what's underneath. The mine spreads it around. The ridge is set in concrete all over the valley. It's rolling around in those trucks. It's in sidewalks downtown. It's under me now, in the foundation. The ridge isn't going away. It's moving. It's everywhere we look. Our ridge makes roads. It follows us through our days.

The Mountain, Winnie

Saint Helens blows steam and ash 36,000 feet. Nothing like '80, but you can see it clear as a bell over the western sky. It's twilight when I get to the Price Chopper and run into Winnie. The first thing that comes out of my mouth is, The mountain just blew. She's a girl from the old neighborhood. We were 12 the first time around. Just coming into our own. And she was something, 12 year old Winnie. Cute as a bug and so clean she squeaked. Today she is with her two young daughters and all three of them, I can see, are unimpressed by my news.

Winnie. It isn't until after the mountain story that I come up with her name. I realize she isn't who I thought she was. How do I know you? As she talks, I slowly come to see we didn't run into each other. She came over to me. My news about the mountain doesn't interest her because she's approached me for a different reason. It's then I get her name. *This is Dan Peters,* she tells her children. *He's the one I've told you about. He's the one with the fort. Him and Donald.* Oh no, it's Winnie.

I can do nothing in defense. I am so surprised by how much she looks like her old self—delicate hands and button eyes, lips in a bow—and chastened by her equally beautiful daughters, that I can't respond. *He's the one who threw rocks at me. He had dirty magazines in his fort and I broke in and threw them all away.* Oh, why, Winnie? The mountain! But it is me at 12 that has become legend. I'm stuck staring down at her two children. They focus on me with fear and disgust in their eyes, and there I am, still wearing the idiot smile from when I thought this was going to be a pleasant reunion, when I thought I had big news, when I didn't know who I was dealing with. It was Donald, I want to shout. He's the one. He was crazy. I was 12, Winnie. So were you. What about you breaking in? How did I become the antagonist? I haven't seen you in fifteen years. How did I become the cautionary tale? What about the goddamned exploding mountain I just told you about?

I keep smiling. I nod. I think of my own daughter at home with her mother. I'm in a hurry to get there. I want my child to see the plume. And I don't want her to be afraid. I want her to be filled with the same wonder I felt twenty-five years ago. But I'm frozen. I inch away. I am not who you remember, Winnie. People change. I wish I could talk her into a new story. Instead, I say, Good to see you again. Say hi to Frank for me. Take care and get some place safe.

Random Lengths

The wood floor has to sit a week before they install it. It's getting used to the house. Red oak. Random lengths. It's stacked behind our couch, bunched together with plastic ties. Half covered with a sheet, our children climb all over it. Where the kitchen was, where the kitchen will be, is obscured by thin plastic held to the walls and ceiling with blue masking tape which weakens as the weekend wears on. Sunday, Whit wakes up crying. Amy calms him in the living room. She has him nearly asleep when the tape peels away. Whit, eyes wide again, says, *Whoa.*

Summer Nights, Yakima

We're heading south on 16th on our way to a concert
in Franklin Park. A chocolate malt from the fountain
and a blanket on the grass. Folding chairs. Shade trees.
Sunset. On our drive, I see police in the middle of the road
just before Ron's Burgers. The officers jump out,
unholster their weapons, and run east.
Two kids play in a fenced yard.
One cop pauses to say something to them.
It's a question. The older kid raises his arm and points
down the alley beside their house. Both cops take off,
guns up. And it's over. We're through Lincoln
and the action is behind us. Did you see that? I ask.
What? The cops. The police officers. *No. Why, what was it?*
I check the kids. Ella and Whit look the other way.

The Air Is Loose,

Ella, four, says from her car seat beside her brother.
It's the end of August and there's a breeze
bearing gauzy seeds across the valley.
We're in the Selah Gap, near the river.
We drive through a cloud of the fluff
just before town. It swirls around us.
The trees are trying to catch the air, Ella says,
the wind is caught in the cottonwoods.

Death Isn't Death

It's right before Christmas. I'm tucking Ella into bed.
Next to the door is a picture of Gran kissing her
three-month-old head. The picture's been up for years
but we don't talk about it. Once in a while, we'll say,

That's Great-Gran. She loved you very much.
This night, Ella looks at the picture and asks,
Great-Gran died, didn't she? Yes.
And I repeat what we say: Death isn't death.

Death is not the end. When people die, they don't go away.
Part of them lives in us, in you. They pass their spirit.
They're in our hearts. When we remember, they're not gone.
And it's physical, too. You have my chin.

I have Grammy's eyes. It's like a tree in the river.
Or the birch they cut down. It's hard and sad,
but it doesn't have to be. Won't always be.
I can tell Ella believes only some of it.

We'd both like more evidence.
The next day at the Selah Library, the selection process
is random. My finger taps the spines of picture books.
I find a new one about our favorite bear.

I open the cover. Just inside is a note—"This book donated
in loving memory of Mary Johnson." I can't talk.
What are the odds. Look, Ella. Look, Whit.
That's your Great-Gran.

We stare at those words together before they start to squirm.
They want the bear looking for a Christmas tree.
They're ready to turn the page.
Ok, I say, here we go.

Little Deaths

for Whit on the Day of the Dead

Last night you were a bee.
Your sister, a horse and rider. I was a bullfrog.
We gathered treats from family and neighbors.
When we were done
you handed out sweetness at our door.
This morning you woke easily then
fell to pieces. You wouldn't let your mom help.
I couldn't stay. I had this class in Tieton.
I carried you around. Took you outside.
Then I had to go. You chased me to the garage,
cried harder as the door came down.
But if it's true that death isn't death,
that we never really go away,
then I haven't gone anywhere.
Then the slow climb behind the apple truck,
first gear up Young's Grade, was not me leaving.
If it's true, then I'm with you now.
Or rather, you're here with me,
in a warehouse just off the town square.
Your sister and mom came in the same car
and we're checking out a sculpture
of a falling down barn raised ten feet off the ground.
Looking at the slats and spaces.
All our shadows mingled on the floor.
I know. It's a stretch for me, too.
It won't stop your crying
and I still wish I was home. But, pretend.
We can wear our costumes inside this old barn,
bullfrog and bumblebee, horse and rider,
and look up at what's there and what isn't.

Honey Dipper

for Amy

She was taken in by the honey man
at the farmer's market. His golden jars.
His homemade labels. When she asked
a simple question, he'd given her a sermon.

He was religious about honey. A true believer
in his product. He'd told her about the evils
of processed honey. His honey was raw.
His bees had been set out in sumac, huckleberry,

and alfalfa, but the honey she settled on was clover.
She had experience with clover. She liked to sit
in the yard while her children played and carefully
pluck it from the grass. She'd place

the shoots between her teeth and strip out
the juice. Here it was, those nights with her children,
that taste in her mouth, distilled. Natural. Bottled
and ready to take home. The honey man

was so persuasive she bought two. She carefully
placed the sun warmed jars under her son's stroller
next to the carrots and beets. The next morning,
she got up first, went to the kitchen and made coffee.

She took out the buckwheat pancake mix.
Two cups mix. Two cups water. One egg.
Two tablespoons of honey. She got a bowl down
and dumped in the first three ingredients. Then,

she reached for the honey. The lid opened easily.
She dipped a spoon into the jar and drew it out
with a slight twist. She held the spoon over the bowl
and watched it land on the batter.

It rested on the surface before sinking
into the mix. It looked like cursive letters.
Like a new alphabet. She could hear her children stir
in their beds but she did not move. Watching the honey drip,

she recalled the vendor's zeal. It was like reading a book
in a dream. She knew they must be her own words
but the letters felt like they had been put down by someone else.
Maybe the apostle at the market could translate.

Maybe he understood this bee script,
this clover tongue. If she could patiently hold her arm still
at the right angle, she might find their whole story
written in the slow language of honey.

Part Two

THE BOATMAN'S DUMP

for Marj Peters, on her birthday, September 24ᵗʰ, 2004

*A swarm of very small, shallow earthquakes began on the morning
of 23 September and peaked about mid-day on 24 September.*
USGS OFFICIAL PRESS RELEASE:
Mount St. Helens Notice of Volcanic Unrest

These two kids, brother and sister, are in paradise.
It's September 1945 and their parents have rented a cabin
from Harry Truman, owner of Spirit Lake Lodge.
The bombs have been dropped.
The sister, my mom, will be ten in two weeks.
The mountain is whole and calm. School rush over,
their father has closed the dry goods store.
It's the first of many trips. They will return for camps
with friends. In the woods, at rest in bunks,
they build a picture so strong that when the mountain
is half gone, some will be unable to return.

This first summer the brother and sister drift all day
in a rented boat on water so clear that everything is visible.
They bait hooks, drop simple lines over the side.
While she fishes, the sister watches herself watch the water.
At the center of the lake, she leans over and sees
outboard motors, cast off and half sunk in the sandy bottom.
It's the boatman's dump.
Her first thought swarms back, *What can be salvaged?*
How can the engines be recovered?
Mom's dream—float the treasure to the surface—is for us.

Home from Work

for Doug Peters

This is old hat.
He's five years younger than I am now.
He is in a white short sleeve shirt.
Top button undone.
Loosened narrow black tie.
He's sitting in a dining room chair
holding me face down in his left hand.
My chest to his palm.
My legs, arms and head hang down.
This is the house in the country.
It's Labor Day, 1968.
I'm brand-new.

What They Did in Old Deer

The further back I go
the more common I become.
My earliest kin were carters.
Caught salmon. Their children
were crofters, simple farmers.
Their children, stuck in Old Deer,
went different directions.
One kept an inn. One sold coffee.
One dealt spirits.
One, a nightwatchman.
Their children did not go far.
They were gameskeepers,
servants to the manor.
Their children sailed away.

Fortune

Ruth's father sold lumber. He saw his family as upper class.
Henry's father was an immigrant farmer from Tonasket.
Ruth's father thought Henry wasn't good enough for her.
Henry, knowing this, did two things.
First, when Ruth's father came to build their house in Seattle,
he left for the summer. Drove around the country by himself.
Then, for seventy years, he built a blue chip portfolio
on teacher's wages. Banks, trains, Boeing.
He subscribed to Forbes, but seldom sold.
He bought and held. He counted his money often,
was slow to pick up the check, and died rich.
Henry handed all of this down to their only child.
By that time, my father had little use for any of it.

Hunting, Regret: One

When Dad was a boy, Grandpa took him from Seattle
to an island in the Sound that had been overrun by rabbits.
They had a rifle. Grandpa had experience with jackrabbits
in the Okanogan. There's a picture of him in his 20s
standing in a field next to his parents' house. He looks as cool
as he's ever looked. Dark clothes against the snow. Collar up,
wool pants tucked into high boots. Steady gaze. Side by side
open under one arm. A jackrabbit three feet long
hanging from his hands. Maybe this was the picture
he held in his head when they set off. Maybe,
remembering the gameskeepers in Old Deer,
it was a skill he felt he should pass down.
They walked all morning before Grandpa spotted a hare
resting in a warren. It wasn't much of a sport,
but Grandpa had Dad sneak up and fire away
with his single shot bolt action .22.
When the sound quieted down, Grandpa reached in
and pulled the animal out. It did not kick or bleed.
It'd been dead for days.

Mr. Webber's Calliope

There is no beautiful voice the day they see her
in a field off Selah Loop. His father drives him
to see her golden pipes when he is six.
Mr. Webber made her himself. Played in parades for years.
The sound of steam through the valves heard for miles.
But here, in this dusty stubble, concrete bricks block the tires.
There is no steam. No Mississippi Queen.
No mother of muses. They walk around gilded circus scenes.
The son cannot see why they've come.
It might never make music again, for all he knows.
After the crack of the dry weeds
and the song of the grasshoppers,
there is only his father's faint whistle under his breath.

Man from Mars

We are journalists on the way to a party.
Our assignment is to take notes,
report back. It's from my dad.
Detached observer. My dad is
the man from Mars come to earth.
The boy in wonder. Recently, he said to me,
brow peaked, full of the joy of the find,
IHOP *is a* real *experience.*

The Tekiu

Dad and I go to Stan's who, despite his slipping health,
drives us to Rimrock. We walk the ramp
over the silty shore of the lake.
Take it out and then in. Run it right up on the trailer.
Stan attaches a strap, winches us into place.
We lock the rails on the keel. Stan's steady the whole way.
He pulls us to flat ground. We lower the mast,
bungee it up, head home.

Stan and Dad bought the boat in 1976.
Named it for a point in Hood Canal.
Stan taught Dad how to sail.
Stan can't go another year.
Dad can't go without Stan.

This is always a sad day, Stan says.
Yeah, but think about the good sail yesterday, says Dad.
We used to be the last boat out, Doug.
Pulling it through the mud. Lodges all closed.
I ask them about Elk Ridge Lodge,
up the other side of the Y.

That's where the guy had the music, Stan says.
That's right, Stan. He had a room he never left
just off the dining room in the main lodge.
Filled the room with audio equipment.
Speakers covered the walls.
He played it loud enough so that everybody could hear,
but he never came out.
Played every type of music, Stan says,
Wonderful music.
I'm telling you, that guy never came out, Dad says.
Speakers covered the walls, didn't they Doug?

In Three Places on All Souls Day

The art is turned away from us
when we enter the gallery's last floor.
We weave between hundreds of black frames,
solemn as headstones, resting
on easels set in uneven rows. As we walk,
we look back at their fronts. No straight path
in or out. No one way from beginning to end.
When we reach the far side,
we turn and see color. We face
what we have just walked through.

They bring in the Book of the Dead and there I am
shivering in the pew next to Dad in St. James on First Hill.
The church is 100. Dad's 70. I'm 37. The priest
is talking into a wireless mic. I write down his words,
Make friends with death.
I look up at a Bose speaker mounted
to an arch and hear: *Each of us has been touched
by death. His mercies have not been spent.*

Dad and I leave before it's over.
We head to a small club in Belltown.
A vibraphone combo picks it up.
The place is dark and full.
We find a table. Drink coffee.
Between songs, we talk. Watch people.
At the end of the set,
Dad pays our bill and we're gone.

Picture Your Father and His Father

for my son's 39th birthday

Two weeks before your second birthday, your father
and his father loaded a white Chevy pickup, a little one,
and went to the dump. In the back, cut grasses,
lavender, mint, Russian Sage, a pitchfork and a broom.
On top of that, your Christmas tree.
All of it, covered by a blue tarp and bungee cords.
Your father drove. His father bought lattes
and came along for the ride.

Some late-winter Sunday when you're grown,
think of your father, nearly 40, his father, newly 73,
and that tree, left outside for six weeks. Picture your father
and his father hauling the leavings of last summer's garden,
drinking hot coffee, untying the load,
and sweeping out the fragrant remains.

My Father's Frame

His joint fell apart, Mom tells me
after Dad's first surgery.
Everything went as planned,
except when they got in there
the doctor realized he needed a larger prosthetic.
So they sent someone to the closet
to get another off the rack, several sizes up.

Your father, Mom says.
It turns out your father is a big man.
They measured him wrong.
He's a big guy, we knew that.
Your father was built to carry more.

Notes on Mahler's Last Notes

After I leave Dad's hospital room,
I walk through the parking lot.
His blood pressure is way down
and he's been sick to his stomach,
but he's resting. Improving, it turns out.
It's dark, around 9, and I'm in my car,
but I can't tell you anything else.
I turn right on Tieton to go home. Radio's on.
Mahler's adagio from his Tenth Symphony is being introduced.
I hear the announcer say dissonance and eternity music.
I don't know shit about classical but she's got my attention.
Her voice continues—It's his final, unfinished piece.
Leave taking work. A farewell to his wife.
The arc of last notes tells us he was not ready
for serenity, not ready to die.
The music starts.
I find a square of paper on the floorboard
and write what I can while I drive.
When I stop under a streetlight
I see the paper is my parents on their wedding day.
I'd made extra copies for their 50th Anniversary a month ago.
They're leaving the church, looking back
through the car's rear window.
Around their smiling kid faces, Mom still in her veil,
I've written: *Dad/Mahler/Adagio/?*

Fire on the Hill: A Story for Dad's 74th Birthday

This is a story about emboli the size of BBs that shot
from your leg to your lungs. It's about ER doctors and heparin.
About near misses and fear. About phone calls and family.
It's about how we can't do much except be thankful and patient.

In the end, the fire on the hill doesn't reach the house.
It starts at the bottom, a kid with matches,
and works its way up. It starts with Amy at work,
Whit deep in a nap. Sirens coming closer.

I'm on the carpet with Ella
when the first truck goes by. In minutes,
before anyone can reach it,
the fire is near the top of the hill.

It is not under control. Double it
and it's at our backdoor. I don't say anything.
I turn on the sprinklers and garden hose.
They rotate in meager half circles.

I think about things I should have done.
I make promises, bargain.
There's hard drives and photo albums.
Marriage and birth certificates.

I call Mom. We might need help getting out.
Ella comes outside and I hold her in my lap.
I try to act cool, but she's scared.
I show her the damp green grass.

The trenchers make their way down the hill
with picks, shovels, heavy coats and rubber boots.
They dig a line in the dirt. I get Whit up.
The pumper trucks knock down the biggest flames.

It takes minutes for the threat to pass
but the hot spot mop up goes on all afternoon.
This spring, the site of the fire, covered by snow,
uncovered by April, looks black.

We've lived here. We've seen it.
The edges creep in each year. The sage reseeds.
The dark circle is erased. The grass grows back
and little by little the hill heals itself.

Montlake Cut, Opening Day

Your wife and three of your children sit in the Tea Room
at the University of Washington Medical Center
while the doctors wire your breast bone together.
Arm chairs in a line, they hold food in their laps,
stare out the windows at the rain.
An hour earlier, the surgeon came into the waiting room.
Everything went well. No induced hypothermia,
no valve replacement, no major arteries.
Just the Dacron patch to fix the aneurism and save your life.

It had been a tense twenty-four hours.
You checked in the morning before.
Your wife was with you the whole time.
Your two daughters and youngest son came later.
You made small talk. Met the nurses.
Flipped between the NCAA championship
and the first baseball game of the season.
The night before your surgery was opening day.

So the next morning, there's your family,
sitting four across like business-class passengers
on a transpacific flight. It hasn't stopped raining.
A hundred yards away boats cruise through the Montlake Cut.
From where they sit, it looks as if they are floating
over the grass. Just below the second story windows
a crew in orange vests is working on an irrigation problem.
One man goes to a valve box in a berm, shuts something off.
It's a burst pipe. The team makes sharp cuts in the sod
with shovels. Piles the green grass to the side.
They spend some time bailing, blades turned to oars.
They expand the hole toward your family.
Find the leak in the line and climb out.
The damaged section is exposed. It's on to replacing it.
Your wife and youngest son sit next to each other in silence.
Once or twice they comment on what's being done.
How hard they're working.
How glad they are to be out of the rain.

Photograph of Your Grandmother in Bend

It's winter, but there's no snow. Five neighborhood kids.
Jackets zipped, hats back on their heads.
My mom, age 4, rides in the pilot seat of the wagon and holds
a shovel like an oar. Gloved hands. She looks content.
You can't see what the boys are holding, but you can see
your grandmother lost in play. Making believe
in the cold air. Warm in her trust of these friends.
Sure of the man who takes her picture.

Hunting, Regret: Two

for Tom

Grandpa Johnson hunted as a boy in Iowa.
There are photos of him in his first year of teaching.
He's in Bainville, Montana, pointing a pistol into a field.
He shot upland birds in Bend when he was the principal.
He opened a dry goods store in Cathlamet,
shot muddy ducks with his son and a friend.
So it was a surprise, Mom said, when he came home
holding a swan. He was beside himself.
He said, *It's illegal. I don't know what happened.*
He took the bird to the basement and placed it
on his workbench. Mom sat on the stairs
and watched his back while he studied what to do next.

Above Quepos

That night the jungle opened up.
A house or hotel appeared between us
and the ocean. It was quiet where we were.
In the distance, a party. Strings of lanterns.
Music drifting over the canopy.
In the daylight, there were only trees and water.
In the dark, maybe a mile away,
something else.

Back home, Amy sees Gran in the hospital.
She tells me, *She knew who I was.*
It's hard. She was honest.
I walk outside. August stars.
Bass from a Civic Center *quinceañera*
floats up, unreachable as
that island of light in the palms.

What Happened Later That Day

in memory of Mary Johnson

Steam rises from the apple juice plant,
slightly sweet from the process.

It ascends in a straight column,
just past the ridgeline,

then nothing.
The mist trails away to blue sky.

Not nothing.
Some clouds. Brown hills.

Our slow breath.

Part Three

THERE'S A BOY ON THE BRIDGE

A young man, behaving violently
walks over the Fred Redmon. No car.
Interstate traffic going by at 75.

He's yelling. It's 7:30 Saturday morning.
He's making his way across the span.
I pull to the side just after the bridge and watch him.

He's wearing a thin cowboy shirt, unbuttoned
and untucked, but he does not look like a cowboy.
He grabs a handful of gravel and throws it at a passing car.

Scrapes up another load and throws it over the bridge.
He tears his shirt off and launches it over the edge as if
it was gravel, too. Then he clutches the rail with both hands,

faces away from the road and screams. His shirt
is three feet out. It's such a sudden sight that he stops
and follows its descent. It will take time

for it to drift the next hundred yards. The screaming
resumes. He's past the middle, if he was looking for it.

Kicked in the Eye

The child rounds the corner of the swing set
and meets the boot of Eric Lee as he speeds upward.

Mrs. Lee wraps the child in her arms.
She presses a kitchen towel to his brow

as she half-walks, half-runs up the street.
She cradles him hard against her chest.

It's dark.

She pulls the towel away, looks in his eyes.
He sees his blood and her fear.

It's bright again.

Drinking the Mirror

Milk and glass pour from my thermos.
The mirror inside, broken, swallowed.
All my friends left to play.
I sit in a dark classroom
with Mrs. Eilers feeding me
slice after slice of bread.

My First Babysitter

once raised her shirt and let me put
my four year old finger in her navel.
She was our minister's daughter. Long, straight
blond hair. Beautiful round face.
After my parents were gone, if we were good, she'd lift
her guitar from its velvet lining,
place the woven hippie strap over her shoulder
and play "Leaving on a Jet Plane."
When my parents came home
she'd snap shut her hourglass case
and kiss us all goodbye.

Re-creations

Whenever he visited his dad's work, after he'd stapled and notarized as many sheets of paper as he cared to, the boy was turned loose in the conference room. The only things to play with were cars and trains stuck on the blackboard. They used them to show scenarios, just before or after accidents. To establish a client's guilt or innocence. They weren't toys. Their magnets were weak and the wheels didn't turn. Even so, the boy would push a chair over and climb up. There were intersections drawn on the board and formulas for stopping distance. Traffic lights, railroad crossings. He made noises as he screeched the figures around the green surface. Smashed them up. He'd spend the afternoon making trains run off tracks, sending cars into corners they couldn't take, picking the pieces off the floor and doing it again. He drove them down the silver chalk tray, coating his hands in fine dust.

When that got old, he'd hop down and visit the basement. *Sunny Jim* in a mini-fridge. On the other side of the kitchenette were the bathrooms. One for Ladies. Flowers in a vase. A lounge chair. The bathroom the boy used was marked Men. The wallpaper was 70s era oranges and blacks. Under the sink, the *Playboys*. After checking to make sure he was alone, the boy would sit in the bathroom, open the cupboard, reach around the waste basket and pull a magazine from the middle of the pile. Barbie Benton. Cartoons. Dandelion fields. Tan lines. Hair. Jokes. Swimming pools. Whiskey ads. Joe Namath. He was old enough to know he shouldn't be doing it. He kept the door closed and was careful to put them back in the same place. It was not exciting the way it would be later. He was curious. From his spot on the floor in the basement of his dad's work, the boy's questions, about where he'd come from and where he was going, were being answered.

Party Line

There were other voices when I picked up
the telephone in my grandmother's house.
Strangers talking about nothing
that would interest a child. Still, I held my breath

and waited for a slip, a secret to be exposed.
It was her only phone, a black rotary with a long cord,
in the center of her small house.   .
I had questions. Gran might have known

who they were or where the voices came from
but I understood I had to stay quiet. I knew
there was no way to ask about the mystery
without revealing the secret and cutting the line.

Gravel

I remember how it was to drive in gravel. Not dirt. Dirt had its own set of values. Dirt was more stable. Dirt was following someone too closely. If it made any sound at all, dirt was a squeak. Steep inclines. It was roll up the windows. Dirt was jackrabbits in front of headlights on the LT Murray and kegs and fires. And not gravel in parking lots or on shoulders or in the oldest parts of town, or driveways, or vacations or the first half mile of logging roads. I mean gravel roads. Or stretches of road that turned to gravel. The rules were different once you left asphalt. The allowances were greater somehow. Gravel was county.

I remember how it was to drive in gravel. It was me and Jeff trashing his sister's EXP on the road between Elks Golf Course and Monson's feedlot, listening to "Cuts Like a Knife" and pulling up hard on the e-brake around corners. Gravel was the back way home. Just as the physics of driving on gravel changed, so did the morality. It was as if the frictionless crunch of the road freed us in other ways. Gravel was alcohol. Gravel was skipping. Gravel was pissing anywhere you cared to. Gravel can't be cleared in winter. Gravel was after the dance.

I remember how it was to drive in gravel. Gravel had a violence that went beyond the noise it made on the quarter-panels. It had been terrible on bikes. Been pulled from elbows, forearms and knees. Even earlier it had been picked up by the handful and used as buckshot between neighbor kids. Its brutality only increased when we started driving.People lost their lives on it. If I ever almost died on gravel, I never knew about it. I trusted it. I still drove too fast. Still loved the sound. Still felt a surge when I hit it as they had, full speed, moving from the uncompromising pavement. Still drank and pissed and parked on it. Still laughed on it. Still punched it from dead stops. Still sought it out. Still counted on its forgiveness.

Fish in the Bucket

But I will put hooks in your jaws
and make the fish of your streams stick to your scales.
I will pull you out from among your streams,
with all the fish sticking to your scales.
      Ezekiel 29:4

We were the worst the camp director had seen. The camp hosts hundreds of kids a week all summer long. During one week in the summer of 1985, the boys from my hometown stood out. Worst ever. In our stay there, we climbed out of our bunks, stole from the kitchen, vandalized rooms, smoked cigars in plain view. Made out with girls from other youth groups. We were 16, 17. We were talked to.

The camp was on the coast of British Columbia. A day's ferry from Vancouver. It was originally a resort. Sand was brought in to create beaches, soil barged in to build a golf course. 1945. Big stars. Now it was led by believers who came of age during the Jesus-Christ-Superstar 70s.

We met in living rooms during the year. Fifty cross-legged, back-rubbing kids. One of the highlights was this camp. We raised money for it the hard way—candy sales, car washes. My friends were sincere. We wanted to be closer to God. We asked questions. We talked to each other. We sang the songs.

One morning, too early for waterskiing, we fooled around with a line and a hook. Brady took out a hidden Walkman and a Boston tape. We pocketed the headphones whenever a counselor came by. Somebody caught something. A trout maybe. Too small. Still we landed it and tried to kill it. There were a handful of us there. We grabbed the tail and swung it like a limp hammer against the planks. That seemed to work. Nobody knew what to do next. Nobody wanted to clean it. The kitchen might cook it for our dinner. We put it in a yellow bucket with a little water at the bottom. One thing led to another and we forgot about it.

The next morning we were back at the dock. It had been almost a day. The fish jumped. Gave the bucket a serious a jerk. We looked closer. It was in terrible shape. Shine gone. Eyes white. But it moved every so often. We got a stone from shore, smaller than a fist, dumped the fish out and hit it again. The twitch was fainter. The life was out of it. We followed the lunch bell back to the lodge. It was time to sing again.

It's the Fourth of July, 1989

We're home from college. It's just after dark. Someone's parents
are gone. Barbeque. Swimming. There's six of us. We've been
drinking. One boy puts down his punk and picks up a bottle rocket.
He's got a beer in the other hand. Another friend says, *Put that
thing in your mouth and I'll light it. Launch that bitch right off your face.*
Everybody thinks this is a good idea. The boy bites down gently
on the stick, leans his head back, closes his eyes, smiles.

Starting on My Left Foot

1.

I open a dorm fridge. A bottle of Blitz rolls out,
shatters on the tile floor. One piece
cuts an inch of my sandaled foot. I pluck it out.

2.

Sophomore year, Selah High.
My fingers find lumps along my right tibia.
I get a biopsy. They're nothing. Calcium.
I watch the doctor stitch it up.

3.

Junior year, Vikings versus Wildcats.
My knee clunks out and back making a block.
ACL, crutches. The whole deal.

4.

I stumble, a little drunk, down a dirt bank
at Bridget's senior party. May 1987.
I'm surprised to be invited and end up posing, bluffing.
First cigarette in my lips. Bigmouth in my hand.
The retaining wall is crumbling or incomplete.
A length of rebar brushes my left thigh below my shorts.
Someone has to tell me, Dan, you're bleeding.

5.

Just above my waist, left side, lower back, barely visible,
a birthmark.

6.

David Haberman ducks his helmet in a tackling drill.
I wrap him up. The whistle blows.
My left bicep is stuck in his facemask.
The coach separates us.
Part of me stays with Haberman.

7.

Right thumb. 1980. Curt's over. My parents are out
and my sister is supposed to be watching us.
We're watching The Hulk save the Cowboys' Cheerleaders.
After the show, Curt and I tear pop cans in half.
It takes a day to stop the bleeding.

8.

Yakima Pallet and Bin. 7 am. 1988.
Tim Maybee and I are fixing pallets.
He holds the pallet on end while I pound in stringers.
My hand is up by the head of the sledge.
I'm hitting the wood as hard as I can.
The hammer glances off the 2 x 4.
The tip of my right index finger pops open.
There's no blood but I'm dizzy and pale.
Dumb, dumb, dumb, I say to myself in wonder.
My boss drives me to the ER.
It's one of my best days on that job.

9.

The back of my left hand, between my thumb and index.
No idea.

10.

I'm crawling. This is in the house in the country.

I tumble down the stairs and land on the corner of
an empty aquarium. Right between my eyes.

11.

On the very top of my head. Again, it's Curt.
We're playing goal line on my parents' bed.
Dad's reading pillow is our blocking dummy.
I've got to get the Nerf into the end zone.
I go low three straight times. It's fourth down.
I've been setting this up. I fake low, then shoot up,
into Curt's chin. We both reel.
I reach up and there's lots of blood.
I run to the kitchen screaming, I've cracked my skull.
Mom cups my head under the kitchen faucet.
The water runs red. *No*, Mom says, *you're going to live.*

Ballard Smoke Shop, Lounge and Café

Three men sit at the unlucky end of the horseshoe.
The one in the middle buys a round.
He is in shirtsleeves and holds a baseball hat in his lap.
The men on either side wear caps and beards.
These two are brothers.
Right testicle and left testicle, one slurs
as they straddle the stools.

On the walls:
Half-won pull-tab prize sheets.
Halloween decorations strung out and stapled.
Black and white photos of fishing boats at sea.
Sockeye, crab, king, stuffed and mounted.

I'm the first-born son of the first-born son
(the other joins in)
of the first born son.
We're talking medieval shit.
I'm the king of my clan.

Patty brings me a can of Bud
and asks, *Do you want a glass?*

I'm the last-born son of the first-born son, the other says.
You still got clout, the first replies.
They finish their drinks standing,
tug at the crotch of their jeans,
find the arms of their coats,
tap packs into their front pockets and make their exit.
One waves while the other leans on the metal bar
and pushes his way onto the street.
Cold air mixes with the smoke and warmth of the lounge.
A minute later, one brother reenters.
I want to apologize for Dave, he tells Patty.
He's a good man, he just don't know what he's talking about.

Across the street at Thaiku
the faux-antiqued walls echo soft electronica
and customers order rounds of Singha.
The guy behind the counter brings a bottle
with a glass and two napkins.
On one napkin he places a second glass
and fills it with ice water and a lemon wedge.

A few blocks down, the locks fill and empty,
change fresh water for salt.

But here at the Smoke Shop, Patty hugs the last-born son.
Forgives whatever sin he confesses
and wishes him goodnight. She goes back to the women
who have come for a tall chablis and a smoke.
Calls thanks to me, too, as I finally swing out the door.

Behind Some Motel in The Dalles

So he walked around the back of the motel.
It was even darker there.
He picked his way through rocks and scrub brush.
He knew he was facing the river.
His eyes began to adjust. His heart slowed a bit.
Just ahead, near where he guessed the cliffs were,
three outbuildings took shape in the blackness.
As he got closer, he could tell they were fishing shacks.
A few empties scattered about but otherwise
they were abandoned.
They leaned there, huddled and useless.

He stared into the night and tried to imagine
what it was like before the dam.
Ropes and nets in the huts.
Men working together above the dalles.

He was calm now and went back in.
He and his father ate in the motel restaurant.
The older brother refused to leave the car.
Their father talked to one then the other
but nothing helped. After dinner,
the father sat in the lobby and the younger brother
found a place in a hallway where he read an article
about the country going to war.
It took his mind off everything else for awhile.

Finally, he gave the keys to his father and stood back.
His father handed the keys to his oldest son
who started the car and went on his way.

After Bodeen's Neruda

From air to air, like an empty net
I went between the streets and atmosphere
arriving and departing.
　　　　Pablo Neruda, "The Heights of Macchu Picchu"

One November morning,
back and forth between home
and the poem, between Selah
and Tieton, between yellow
and brown, I see two things
that make me think of you.

On the way out, blackbirds
leap from an overgrown
fruit-heavy crabapple tree.
Driving back, a man
walks a busy stretch of Highway 12,
new rake, bright red teeth,
slung over his shoulder like a rifle.

Meat

The woman to my right waits for her fried chicken
at the supermarket deli counter.
One of the women who work there calls me sir.
The other woman who works there chuckles. *Sir.*
Both over fifty. The one who laughs says,
They should call us ma'am. Isn't that right?
Sir. Have you heard that before?
she asks as she hands over the breasts and thighs.
The woman to my right grabs the sack, says,
I've heard just about everything. Everyone laughs
as the woman who called me sir puts my meat on the scale.

Dream After *Monster*

It's a Christmas Parade. Fire Engines.
Lights strung on trucks.
The drill team is filled with women I have hurt.
I stand in the middle of their ranks,
tell them what I've done about it.
They listen as they dance by. They forgive me.
I turn in the night to face another and another.

Brittle

I make my friends candy
but I do not give it away.
I melt sugar, crush nuts,
cool it and crack it.
I heat bitter cocoa
with heavy cream,
roll it in sweet chocolate,
freeze it until it grows stale.
I wrap it in wax paper,
put it in tins and it sits.
Mine. I eat until my teeth
hurt. Until it goes bad.

Driving Home Two Days Before Thanksgiving After a Faculty Meeting Called to Discuss Twenty to Thirty Percent Budget Cuts for Next Year

He wanted to cross as much water as he could, so he took Highway 12 home. He needed the time. This goddamn fall, he said out loud as he drove. He'd turned 40 at the end of summer. Ever since, it had been a plunge. There'd been pink eye, laryngitis, coughing all night, no sleep, hernias, nightmares, hospital visits to his dad, a broken rib, viruses. His 401k was halved. His sister lived next to a house in Portland that had simply slid right off the hillside. The whole country was in deep shit and he was at a loss. The man watched the sunlight fade on Mount Clemens and said to himself, It's beautiful, but it didn't help. He was not angry, he was worried. But it wouldn't take much to set him off. His dad, who had been through a lot that fall himself, much more than the man, had called to ask him how he was doing. The man was ready to blow. He hadn't had a drink in five years but he wanted a beer. Earlier, when someone asked the president how much they'd save if they took a huge pay cut, she said, *As a matter of fact, I have those numbers here*, and read them from the back of an envelope. At the end of the meeting some people clapped. They clapped. He did not feel pity for his colleagues, his students, his father and mother, his wife or himself. He knew how to be an adult. But this was different. It was all at once and so close to his birthday. He was being tested. They all were. Things were stacking up and there was no help coming. People had their own problems. If he was going to get through it, the man would have to untie these things. He knew that. He'd be better off if he looked at them one at a time. Not make a list out of them. But it wasn't so easy. Everything had become a sign. The signs had begun to look like a pattern. And this pattern made the man want to ask strangers, What're you smiling at?

Nobody Does Anything About It

Ella won't stop talking about spring.
Someone told her about spring fever
and now she won't let it go.
Street sweepers come out to gather gravel

and she says, *Looks like somebody's got
spring fever.* We plant seeds in peat pots,
set them in the kitchen sill.
She pours water over the dirt.

She sees green poppy leaves left from
a late fall burst and insists it's new growth.
When I tell her I don't think so, I'm the one
who's wrong. She claims she overheated

at recess and had to take her hat off. I remind her
it's 40 degrees and with the wind it's more like,
Hell no, I'm not going out there
to make fairy homes from dried sunflowers.

Have at it. I'll watch from the doorway.
Every afternoon when I drag myself home
she's there, bellyaching about the weather,
as if I make the wind blow or not,

as if I can make the sun melt the ground,
as if I control the tilt of the earth's axis,
as if I'm the reason it's cold.

Agitator

The old pillow
explodes in the wash.
Wet down
rims the basin,
covers the agitator.
I scoop the trap,
press the feathers
into a ball.

Cavity

There was no light until the end.
They had to drill.
I put on sunglasses, folded my hands
and listened to the whine over the talk
between the doctor and his assistant.
I felt nothing.
They passed instruments back and forth,
once, using my chest as a table.
I stared at the speaker in the ceiling and kept quiet.
I opened up. Tried to give them room to work.
Finally, when the dam came down,
the doctor reached in with a small round mirror
and I saw light reflected from the overhead lamp
flashing in his latexed hand.
A butterfly, there in his palm.
The doctor left me with a pat.
His assistant finished me off,
curing what had been a hole.
My mouth glowed with blue light.
I couldn't speak right for hours.

Punch List

The door to our house is still twisted.
The new floor slopes down.
The glass on this cabinet is scratched.
There are gaps between the counter and the wall.
The stove sticks out.
We think the hood vents into the kitchen.
Hardware's missing from the file drawers.
The paint needs touching up
and we need one more pull.

Jim Says,

There are ways to see this
bigger than we do.
We're only seeing a small part of it.

I nod. Unsure.
I am seeing it small.
There are ways to see it bigger.

I would if I could, Jim.
You'd show me if you could.
But you can't and I don't.

I've got some questions, I say.
I'll ask them when we talk.
They can wait.

Jim won't. He asks,
What about those questions?

I Come from Old Deer

I can go back eight generations
to George to John to Alexander Sr.
to Alexander Jr. to Henry to Doug
to me to Ella and Whit.
Four here. Four there.
I can go back
to Old Bridge of Don, Cruden,
to Stuartfield, Old Deer,
to New Machar Parish, Aberdeenshire,
to Village of Stuartfield, Forres Parish,
to Morayshire, Brae of Biffie,
to Aden, South and East Lodge, Peterhead,
to Glasgow, New York,
to Lincoln Township, Estherville,
to Emmet County Iowa, Minnesota,
to Post Falls, Hauser, Kootenai County Idaho,
to Seattle, Yakima,
to Selah.

The Natural Space Between the Bones

for Eric

is missing. Both you and me. The small muscles,
the tissue, maybe the heart, fouled up.
Something not working in the joints, the gaps.
Thanks, then, for talking today and last year.
There are ways to keep the body from freezing.
Ways to keep a hold. That's one.

The Florian Gate

We made love in the first class cabin. It was downhill after that. First, we got kicked out of our sleeper just over the Czech-Polish border. Then the passport inspectors wouldn't let us rest. Finally, in the middle of the night and without warning, we had to switch cars to avoid going to Warsaw. We ended up in Krakow at 5:30 am with maybe three hours sleep.

The Krakow station is an ugly place at 5:30. After an hour wait we got on a train to the town of Oswiecim. It took another two hours of bouncing along the tracks with commuters to go the last fifty kilometers. Once there, we waited an hour for a bus. The bus dropped a ways from the museum at about 9 am—twelve hours after we left Prague.

We trudged to the entrance across a vacant field. We stopped at the camp gift shop and looked at some postcards. In the cafeteria, once the camp's processing center, we slid plastic trays along a buffet, ate from red and white paper bowls and sat to rest before going in. It was cold. The snow was to the tops of our boots. Inside the barracks you could see your breath. There were mountains of shoes, combs, brushes, suitcases, glasses. And hair, some still in braids. There was the wall where prisoners were shot. There was the muster area. The crematorium. The interpretative plaques were in Polish and weren't much help. There wasn't much explanation for any of it.

We walked unguided through the grounds. Being so close to the holidays, it was almost empty except for a group of Polish elementary school students. They followed us through the camp. We didn't see much of them, but we heard their voices echo in the rooms behind us. We could hear their shuffling feet. Here and there, the teacher gathered them for a talk. The rest of the time they chattered, skipped or ran. There was some laughter.

We were back at the station by 11:30. The next train to Krakow wasn't until 2 pm. In the waiting room, we sat around with teenagers returning home from school. Slept lightly during the return trip to Krakow and awoke each time in a panic.

Once off the train, we walked two blocks and ran into the Florian Gate, the only one left of eight that served as fortification 1,000 years ago. We turned a corner and everything was better. Once inside the wall, the grim station and dour expressions gave way to packed streets, musicians, food, Christmas lights everywhere, stores of all kinds on either side. This was the Royal Way. We walked through the square and up a block to our hotel. After checking in and cleaning up, we looked around the stalls of the Christmas market that filled the old mill. That night we ate at the finest restaurant in Krakow. We ordered appetizers, salads, main dishes and desserts, wine and beer. I was full to bursting. We ate course after course and paid little in return.

Part Four

General Awareness

I wait patiently with my cart in recessed lights.
Ella in the top, Whit in the basket.
Two teenage boys block my way.
They are goofing around.
Their dad notices me first.
He hits one on the arm and says,
Look out there.
We walk by and stop to look up at the display.
He says, *General awareness, guys.*
This is exactly what I've been talking about.
You need to practice general awareness.
The boys nod.
We go back to what we were doing before.

Charged Objects in a Strange Neighborhood

I can't sleep so I walk.
I stop at a bend in the road
short of the transmission towers
that crest the ridge and run downhill
through a swath of cleared land, over I-5
and disappear into East Marginal Way.
Back near the top, a gray house
older than the sagging lines,
cringes at the edge of the easement.
On the other side of the strip,
about forty yards ahead, a big dog goes insane.
Barks harder and harder. Ok, dog. I hear you.
But there's something going on I can't see.
A field I don't want to cross. I turn around.
The dog trots after me, pissed, yet
even he won't pass under these wires.
Back at my friends', people are getting up.
A white crow glides through the backyard,
lands on the fence. My friends says
it's been around for a couple of weeks.
Maybe it's been through those lines.
Maybe it's the cure.

Trying to Remember

for Brandi

My parents stop by and we talk about Uncle Hal's stroke, a week earlier. We're sitting around our kitchen table. Dad says, *I mean, it's kind of incredible. One minute Hal's driving home through Utah and the next,*—he brings his hand down—*your life's changed.* Chris calls five minutes later with your news.

I tell Amy I have to go for a walk. It's shock. Whatever chemical it is that dumps into my bloodstream makes me feel like I am being carried around my neighborhood in a bubble. I can't get the dazzle out of my eyes. I tell myself to be aware, like I might be asked to testify. I can't be relied on to remember so I take paper and a pen. There's nothing I see on my walk that stands out. I'm home and still not thinking straight. Walk or sit still. Pay attention to what's happening.

I sit at the edge of our lawn and look around the field in front of our house. Our neighbor's Christmas tree, rusty and bare, just beyond the mound of grass clippings. Last fall we had guys take out the western Hemlock just over our hedge. They spent a couple of days chopping and hauling. Dumped poison on the stump and told me not to let our kids near it. The area they'd worked on was bare. Nothing but wood chips and herbicide. But at the edge of the old tree's shadow, there was growth. Underground runners rerouted and coming back through the matte of earth and leaves. The poison hasn't finished it off. There's sagebrush, yellow and purple wildflowers, the lilac still in bloom. Car sounds on 82. Misting rain. Dark in the trees at the bottom of the hill. A deeper light.

Planting Her Garden

for Rob

The garden was the easy part.
Waiting for Brandy to come home from the hospital
was something else. This isn't about the garden.
It was nothing digging in the rich soil on that warm day.
The weeds came right up. The plants went right in.
Still, my dad and I left early. We were going over the pass.
He enjoyed good company, your dad talked Roosevelt baseball,
but he'd sat under your apple trees long enough.
We got in his car and drove by the kids dealing on the corner,
down the winding road, past the storage place
and onto the busy highway. We were less than an exit away,
when I felt for my wallet and found it gone.
Left behind. We took the next off ramp. We were lost.
I drove around some tough parts of Tukwila.
Then there was this two lane road, climbing to the west.
It looked right, but it was a guess.
Suddenly, we were in a forest.

The Duwamish watershed on the back side of your ridge.
It's all fouled up later on, I know. Filled with toxic shit.
But here the trees were lush and the ferns large.
The light broken in cool greens. It was a short passage
of shade where the water drains the other half of your hill,
where coho, Chinook and steelhead grow strong
before they make their run through all
the ugliness—poison they'll have to fight to return—
downriver into Elliott Bay and open water.
When we finally found your house, I ran in,
grabbed my wallet and looked out back.
There you were, in the middle of friends,
shovels turning soil, strong backs, many hands ready to lift.
Working to make a way for your love to come home.

A/B

At the end of the cassette,
seconds, sometimes longer.

Not the inch at the very end,
barren, unrecordable. Before that.

The blank after the last note. Left to run,
you might not recall you'd been listening.

You could go on in this quiet,
forgetting, until a sudden click

ends the barely audible hiss of unused time.
Black tape run out.

I Told You to Find Thin Ice

before I knew it would find me at the cemetery.
We were throwing bread
to the ducks that live there year round.
At the far end of the pond, ice,
like a sheet pulled part way over a bed.
Water resting on the surface of water.
The edge, a shore, rising and falling.

Closing the Pool

Winter Solstice

Keep the valve open
with your teeth,
rubber stem free
in your mouth.
Late spring released
in late summer.
Late summer remembered
in deep winter
like an ice core.
Press against it
with your weight,
until you are lying on its length,
embracing, the exhale louder
as you lunge. Pull tighter.
Empty all four chambers.
Feel the air blow back
in your mouth.
What comes out—
what once surrounded it.

There Were Orchards on Those Ridges

There were orchards on those ridges
the man remembers, driving home from work.
The orchardists tore them out and sold them
to richer orchardists. The richer orchardists put
huge houses on those ridges. One of the houses
has a square of trees, out in front.

I Keep a List in My Head

of times I've seen that kid.
Walking down 1ˢᵗ, or Wenas.
Today, January 20, my daughter's second birthday,
he's in a blue tank top, beat up Raiders hat,
pulled down to the bridge of his nose.
Under it, wrap-around gas station sunglasses.
Greying denim shorts, pushed low.
Hands as deep as they'll go in his empty pockets.

Earth Day, 2007

The man who, twenty-five years ago, posted a sign that said
"Vote No" on the school bond is in his driveway.
He's bent over, hitting a weed with Roundup.
He pumps the handle twenty times. Moves to the next.

Across from 7-11

They tore down a hundred year old church.
Replaced it with an eight hole strip mall.
A check cashing oufit, Uncle Bucks.
Then, seven empty spots.

Warplane Strafes School

found in The New York Times *the day after the election, 2004*

The warplane, flying a night training mission, fired a burst
as it streaked over Little Egg Harbor.
The one-story school on Frog Pond Road
was unoccupied except for the night custodial staff.
It sounded like somebody running across the roof of the school,
said the cleaning woman. Custodians found 13 lead slugs
more than 2 inches long. There were holes in in the ceilings and
floors of several classrooms. At least one desk was hit.
We have no idea why the gun went off, the colonel said.
It was not an intentional release.

Snake Head

I was feeding the horses.
A rattler came into the corral. Five footer.
I pinned it with an irrigation pipe.
Got a shovel and cut off the head.
When I went to grab it, it raised up,
did a back flip almost, and got my finger.
Just the head.
I had to shake my hand hard to get it to let loose.
By the time we got to the hospital
my tongue was swollen twice its size.
I asked myself, How'd that happened? What'd I do?
They rushed me to Richland in an ambulance.
Took six shots to stop the poison.
When I got back to the house, I found the head
where it landed, in the bed of the truck.
I'd do it again, do it over. Use the same shovel.
Only, I'd turn up some dirt with the blade.
Put that son-of-a-bitch in a hole right then.
Stick that head in the ground for good.

Transport, April 2008

The convoy crests Snoqualmie Pass.
Toward the front of a blue school bus,
a soldier in desert fatigues
leans to look out his window
at the snow and the mountains.

The William O. Douglas Pay Phone

The day after McCain accepts the Republican nomination
under the banner of Country First and in front of a screen
showing flight suits, Hanoi, coming home, the man
is in the woods celebrating his 40th birthday
and his 13th anniversary with his wife.
After dinner at the lodge, his wife walks back to the cabin
and the man stops to call his parents from a pay phone outside.
There's music in the bar, noise from the road.
The man asks his dad, How are the kids holding up?
He can barely hear the answer. It's like talking
over two way radios. He tells his dad to speak up.
His dad says, *Where are you calling from?*
Did you know that's a famous phone? They say
William O. Douglas stopped Nixon from bombing Cambodia
from that phone. 1970. About this time of year.
There ought to be a plaque above it, the man jokes.
He hangs up, steps into the minimart.
Next to the freezer case is a paper stand.
McCain's saluting on the front page.
As he waits to get rung up,
the man looks at the hand that held the receiver.
I would've been two, my son's age.
I didn't know anything.
He holds out his hand to receive the change from the clerk.
He wants to call his dad back, thank him for the story
and for looking after his children, but he doesn't.
They're probably getting ready for bed.
He walks past the phone and down the hill to his cabin,
a milkshake in each hand.

Rebuilding the Lincoln

for Ella's fifth birthday, January 20th, 2009

We're watching the Inaugural Concert with our son and daughter.
They seem disinterested. Obama is about to speak.
They're playing with blocks.

Ella says, *I'm making where that guy's talking. Look at that.*
Did you see that picture of the building?
The building is what I made.

We look and, sure enough, they've recreated the Lincoln Memorial
in our living room. A Neo-Classical Doric temple
out of wood blocks.

They're working together, brother and sister. It's their idea.
I'll make the Reflecting Pool, Ella says. Whit says,
There's some blocks.

Boots

Your friend leaves a message. *I've got these barely worn boots,* he says. *Size 11. You want them? Call me back.* They're a size small you tell him when you do. Why are you getting rid of them? *I don't know. They just don't work for my feet. That ever happen to you?* Yeah, sure, you say. But these are the only shoes you'll wear. You swear by the brand to this very man who now finds he can't wear them. He's your mentor, a brother. Yet, he can't walk in your boots and you can't walk in his. It's a waste. It doesn't seem possible. *I'll wear them on a hike sometime,* he says, *and leave them in the woods.*

Microcosm

for BG

There is no way to mark this.
It would take a movie the length
of 6,000 school days, probably, to capture it.
But, told right, the moment may stand in.

1986. Twenty years ago this April, you wrote
microcosm on the chalkboard and I put it in my notebook.
Thick chalk banging, you drew a large circle,
then a small one. You said, *Little world. Big world.*

I wrote those four words. That's what comes back.
How the lesson started.

On the First Night of Class Karelys Beltran, Who Wants Me to Say Her Name Right, Whose Name I Will Learn to Say, Asks *What Do You Want to Be Remembered For?*

I stumble and fuck up
my answer about teaching.

Get thrown and come up empty
when I talk about home.

I wish I'd don't speak my name for a year after I'm gone.
I wish I'd said bring strong coffee and sagebrush to my grave.

I wish I'd said the true teacher knocks down the idol.
I wish I'd said don't look at the finger pointing to the moon.

I should've said I hope my children remember a warm house.
I hope they remember me being around.

I didn't get the answer right because
I'm a beginner. A slow learner.

Too much hanging on.

Because I'm in denial.
Because I remember Tom Pier.

Because Karelys surprised me.
Because it's none of my business.

All of this comes to me late.
Early the next morning. Not too late.

Letter To Students Who Are Not Here

in memory of Karen, Jessica, and Jason

Words and books
Like a small creek off a high ledge
Gone in the dry air.
                  Gary Snyder, "Piute Creek"

The hills are green and will be for a month.
Then, as the cheatgrass matures, they will turn red.
By the time you come home, fewer than before,
they will have changed to various shades of brown.
Now, though, they are green and some mornings,
when clouds cover the valley, you can squint your eyes
and almost believe you are in another country
where all year long, hills remain
as round and bright as these ridges today.

A year ago, I wrote another letter.
I said I don't have anything other than easy answers
that seem tired before I can get them out of my mouth.
Much later, I saw some things were passing through me.
Maybe it was just so much had changed.
My friend drove me around for more than an hour.
He copied down this line: *No one loves rock, yet here we are.*

Outside my window the sound of a lawnmower
drifts back and forth. I am not where I was,
and you are not here, anymore.
The ridges change as they did before any of this happened,
before we lost so much.
That's no kind of answer, but I'll stand by it.
Across the valley, I can see pillars of smoke
where orchards stood. The trees behind your school
empty of blossoms in the wind and rain.
Those beside the river fill with leaves.

Piano for the Left Hand

It was a fluke he was there. The man had never been to a symphony and here he was at Benaroya Hall in Seattle. He'd come over with his wife, who was taking night classes at the U.W. Usually, he'd drop her off and then do something downtown. This night, he had dinner in the bar of Wild Ginger, a hip fusion place, then thought, I'll walk over to Benaroya. See what's going on. He bought a cheap ticket way up in the balcony and went in.

The program started with *Piano Concerto for the Left Hand*, by Ravel. The pianist, Leon Fleisher, had been a prodigy but a crippling illness limited his right hand, so he became a master of this unusual piece. The music was dark. All those bass notes within easy reach. Fleisher turned pages with his right hand, but otherwise it rested at his side. It started slowly, increased intensity then slowed again. The man was fascinated. He identified with the music. He liked the strangeness of it. He was left handed and drawn to the rumble of the low notes. The darker the better.

After intermission, the Lyon orchestra played Stravinsky's *Rite of Spring*. The program explained it as a vision of a girl dancing herself to death in a pagan ritual. When it was first performed, a riot broke out. The man settled into his seat.

Halfway through the first movement, the man started to cry. It came out of nowhere and at first, he was self-conscious. He thought, maybe I'm forcing this. Maybe I'm trying too hard. But then he leaned forward and rested his chin in his hands and couldn't stop. When he asked himself What was it? he thought of a former student who had died suddenly on a mission trip to South America. The man had put this death out of his mind. Now spring is coming and Jason's not here. But that had been over a year ago and it wasn't what set him off. It wasn't grief that made the man cry.

After the performance he walked several blocks to his car. It was a cold, wet night and the air felt good. He drove north, just in time to meet his wife coming out of class. What'd you do tonight? she asked. The man tried to explain. He started at the beginning and it didn't add up. He shook his head. He was embarrassed. The man couldn't say what had washed over him. He couldn't say why.

We Hold Hands

My right hand is swollen at the base of the middle finger. I feel it as I type. No one could say what was wrong. I approached the reception desk and a stone-faced woman handed me paperwork. After a long time, a nurse called me back. *What are you here for?* She made an x on a diagram of a knuckle in my folder. She picked up my hand, turned it over and pressed where it hurt. She let go of my hand, asked about the pain. *Date of birth? Married? Do you have any children? Ages? Where do you work?* I told her. *What do you do there?* I'm a teacher. She marked it in my chart. I stared at the top of her head. *What subject?* English. Her pen stopped. She checked my name and something happened. She looked up. Did you teach at West Valley? Yes. *I'm Jason Swift's mom.*

I've been meaning to write you. You were important to him. She begins to cry. I say, Jason was not like other kids. We made a connection. I think about him all the time. When I see his friends. When I teach. *Yes,* she says. Her composure, gone. *He'd come home and talk about your class.* We are far away from the doctor's office. I tell her how sorry I am. How hard it hit me. *He* was *different,* she says but can't continue. I tell her about Jason coming in after school. About the respect of teachers and students. About his humor. About Dave Matthews and the Counting Crows CDs he made for me. About his time in Jackson Hole with his sister. I tell her about Liz. How badly his friends miss him. *Well,* she says trying to get it back, *I've been meaning to write you a note. I wanted to tell you how much you meant to him.* She apologizes for her emotions. He was sweet and kind, I tell her. He was special. She holds my hand again, briefly. *Yes,* she says. *Thank you. I'm glad to finally meet. Good to put a face to a name.*

Blueberries and Ribs

for Linwood Powell, home from Iraq

Everything's gone.
I got a stomach full of ribs.
Took some to my friend from North Dakota,
the one who brags on his recipe,
the one who's seen war, too. He called and said,
Your friend can cook.
Kept a few for Dad. Amy had some.
Everyone got a taste.
And it was so good. The smoke
and easy peel of the pig. When the last rib
was clean, I collected everything in tin foil,
set the bones in the can outside
and thought of your family.

Nothing's gone.
We ate the last of the blueberries on New Year's Day,
frozen from a summer U-Pick in Naches.
It was word of mouth at Amy's work. Someone said,
Blueberries this weekend. That's how people knew.
Mennonite women, bonnets and skirts,
directed cars to a parking lot in a field.
Families came and went. Sun low in the sky.
We were given buckets, led down a row and told,
This is your spot.
Ella ate as much as she picked. Whit rested in his car seat.
We gathered gallons. Enough to make pancakes
and pies and cobbler. Enough to have blueberries
with ice cream at night and on cereal in the morning.
We turned cream blue.
They've kept me thinking about summer,
about when things will warm back up.

I'm not close to saying what it was like, Linwood.
Or what it has to do with manhole covers you can't drive over.
Or the beret you brought home and threw away.

But out in Naches, on the old highway
just over the hill from home, there's this abundance.
This ease. We comb the bushes
and berries spill from our hands by the hundreds.

ACKNOWLEDGMENTS

Thanks to Amy Peters for her help.

Thanks to Rod Peters, Heather Magruder and Sally Gray for leading the way down the road.

Thanks to Jim and Karen Bodeen.

Thanks to Barry Grimes.

Thanks to Robert Fisher.

Thanks to Kathleen Flenniken and Joe Stroud.

Thanks to Kevin Miller for encouraging me to put these poems together.

Thanks to Carolyn Calhoon-Dillahunt for her close eye.

Thanks to Brett Dillahunt, Jeremy Gaulke, Doug Johnson, Jenifer Browne-Lawrence, Marty Lovins, Terry Martin, Brooke Matson, Josh McKimmey, Tom Moore, Keely Murphy, Linda Pier, Walter Schlect, Derek Sheffield, my students, and especially to Sue and Brian Swift, for commenting on the poems as they were being written and in some cases sending poems and letters back.

Friends, all.

The epigraph comes from "Fried Sausage," an essay by Charles Simic, which appeared in *The Ohio Review,* Winter, 1991. Thanks to Selah Librarian Michael Martin for helping me find it.

"Bird in My Hand," "Skunk in the Well" and "Letter to Students Who Are Not Here" were published in *Weathered Pages: The Poetry Pole,* Blue Begonia Press, 2005.

The line, "notice six things a day" is from the poet Linda Gregg.

"Two Red Peppers" and "Meat" were awarded second place and published in the *Allied Arts Juried Poetry Competition Chapbook*, 2006.

"My Brother's Closet" was first published on the Poetry Pole.

Thanks to Selma Umbarger for donating *Bear Stays Up for Christmas*, the book mentioned in "Death Isn't Death," in memory of my grandmother, Mary Johnson.

"Little Deaths" is a phrase borrowed from section three of Pablo Neruda's poem, "The Heights of Macchu Picchu," with thanks to Jim Bodeen's Latino Literature curriculum.

Information in "What They Did in Old Deer" and "I Come from Old Deer" is borrowed from genealogical work done by LaVere Peters. (http://freepages.genealogy.rootsweb.ancestry.com/~lavere/)

The poem "Gravel" borrows the refrain from the second section of Theodore Roethke's "Journey to the Interior."

The title "Dream After *Monster*" refers to the 2003 film staring Charlize Theron.

The title "Nobody Does Anything About It" is borrowed from Mark Twain's famous statement, "Everybody talks about the weather, but nobody does anything about it."

"The Florian Gate" was awarded Honorable Mention in the 2007 Allen Ginsburg Poetry Award and published in the *Paterson Literary Review*, Number 37.

ARTIST'S STATEMENT

Western art has traditionally encompassed four "landscapes" wherein a region of human understanding is encountered, explored, colonized and pacified. These are the landscape of the psyche, the landscape of the body, the landscape of human action, and the landscape of nature.

A strong formalist education at the University of Washington and Central Washington University prepared me to look at the landscape as considerably more than a decorative or aesthetic backdrop. My work centers on the landscape of nature because in it the other three landscapes are present. For me, understanding nature is understanding myself.

Robert Fisher

Dan Peters was born in 1968. He is a teacher at Yakima Valley Community College. His previous books are *In the Easement of Absent Ties* (chapbook, Blue Begonia Press 1998) and *The Reservoir* (Blue Begonia Press, 2002). He also co-edited the anthology, *Weathered Pages: The Poetry Pole* (Blue Begonia Press, 2005). Peters lives in Selah, Washington with his wife and two children.